To Susan — Merry Christmas 1974 —
With thanks —

Wm Harmon

Sphere

The Form of a Motion

By the same author

Ommateum
Expressions of Sea Level
Corsons Inlet
Tape for the Turn of the Year
Northfield Poems
Selected Poems
Uplands
Briefings
Collected Poems: 1951–1971

Sphere

The Form of a Motion

A. R. AMMONS

W · W · NORTON & COMPANY · INC ·

NEW YORK

This book is set in Linotype Janson. Composition and manufacturing were done by The Vail-Ballou Press, Inc.

First Edition

Published simultaneously in Canada
by George J. McLeod Limited, Toronto
PRINTED IN THE UNITED STATES OF AMERICA

Library of Congress Cataloging in Publication Data
Ammons, A R 1926–
Sphere: the form of a motion.
Poem.
I. Title.
PS3501.M6S6 811'.5'4 74-8124
ISBN 0-393-04388-6
ISBN 0-393-04393-2 (pbk.)

1 2 3 4 5 6 7 8 9 0

For Harold Bloom

I went to the summit and stood in the high nakedness:
the wind tore about this
way and that in confusion and its speech could not
get through to me nor could I address it:
still I said as if to the alien in myself
        I do not speak to the wind now:
for having been brought this far by nature I have been
brought out of nature
and nothing here shows me the image of myself:
for the word *tree* I have been shown a tree
and for the word *rock* I have been shown a rock,
for stream, for cloud, for star
this place has provided firm implication and answering
        but where here is the image for *longing:*
so I touched the rocks, their interesting crusts:
I flaked the bark of stunt-fir:
I looked into space and into the sun
and nothing answered my word *longing:*
        goodbye, I said, goodbye, nature so grand and
reticent, your tongues are healed up into their own
element
and as you have shut up you have shut me out: I am
as foreign here as if I had landed, a visitor:
so I went back down and gathered mud
and with my hands made an image for *longing:*
        I took the image to the summit: first
I set it here, on the top rock, but it completed
nothing: then I set it there among the tiny firs
but it would not fit:
so I returned to the city and built a house to set
the image in
and men came into my house and said
        that is an image for *longing*
and nothing will ever be the same again

Acknowledgments

Sections 1 through 10 of this poem first appeared in *Diacritics*, Winter 1973, Vol. III, No. 4. My thanks for permission to reprint to the editor, David Grossvogel.

Sections 71 and 72 appeared under the title "Providences" in *Granite*, Spring 1974. My thanks for permission to reprint to the editor, Anselm Parlatore.

I acknowledge with special pleasure and gratitude a faculty fellowship provided by the Society for the Humanities at Cornell University which enabled me to work for a year in the old Andrew D. White house and to finish this poem.

Sphere

The Form of a Motion

1

The sexual basis of all things rare is really apparent
and fools crop up where angels are mere disguises:
a penetrating eye (insight), a penetrating tongue (ah),

a penetrating penis and withal a penetrating mind,
integration's consummation: a com- or intermingling of parts,
heterocosm joyous, opposite motions away and toward

along a common line, the in-depth knowledge (a dilly),
the concentration and projection (firmly energized) and
the ecstasy, the pay off, the play out, the expended

nexus nodding, the flurry, cell spray, finish, the
haploid hungering after the diploid condition: the reconciler
of opposites, commencement, proliferation, ontogeny:

2

often those who are not good for much else turn to thought
and it's just great, part of the grand possibility, that
thought is there to turn to: camouflagy thought flushed

out of the bush, seen vaguely as potential form, and
pursued, pursued and perceived, declared: the savored
form, the known possession, knowledge carnal knowledge:

the seizure, the satiation: the heavy jaguar takes the
burro down for a foreleg or so: then, the lighter,
though still heavy, vultures pull and gulp: then, the

tight-bodied black crows peck and scratch: then ants
come out and run around the structure, picking bits:
finally, least bacteria boil the last grease mild:

3

so the lessening transformers arrive at the subtle condition
fine, the spiritual burro braying free, overwhelming
the hairy, and so must we all approach the fine, our

skinny house perpetual, where in total diminishment we will
last, elemental and irreducible, the matter of the universe:
slosh, slosh: vulnerability is merely intermediate: beyond

the autopsy and the worm, the blood cell, protein, amino acid,
the nervous atom spins and shines unsmirched: the total,
necessary arrival, the final victory, utterly the total loss:

we're haplessly one way the wrong way on the runway:
conglomerates, tongues or eyes or heel strings that
keep us, won't keep: we want to change without changing

4

out of change: actually, the imagination works pretty
diagrammatically into paradigm so one can "see things":
and then talk fairly tirelessly without going astray or

asunder: for me, for example, the one-many problem figures
out as an isoceles triangle (base: diversity and peak: unity)
or, even, equilateral, some rigor of rising: and this is

not to be distinguished from the center-periphery thing, in
that if you cut out a piece of pie from the center-periphery
circle, you have a triangle, a little rocky, but if you

cut off the arc, it sits up good, as (peak: center: unity)
and (base: periphery: diversity): actually, one could go even
so far as (peak: center: symbol: abstraction), etc., and the other:

5

this works in the bedrock, too, or undifferentiated gas:
one feels up the two legs of the possibility and, ever
tightening and steered, rises to the crux, to find

there the whole mystery, the lush squeeze, the centering
and prolongation: so much so that the final stone
never locks the peak but inlet: outlet opens unfolding

into nothingness's complete possibility, the strangling
through into the darkness of futurity: it is hard at this
point to avoid some feeling, however abstract the circumstance:

if one can get far enough this way where imagination
and flesh strive together in shocking splendors, one can
forget that sensibility is sometimes dissociated and come:

6

I wouldn't be surprised if the radiance we talk about isn't
that part of the structureless lust that rising from the
depths gets by all the mechanisms of mediation and, left over,

feels like religion, the heights visited; that is, the route
from energy to energy without frigging, an untainted source
with an untainted end: when the professor rises to require

structure in the compositions, he invokes a woman: he wants
shapeliness intact, figure shown forth: dirty old
man hawking order and clarity: but if he would not

be dark, what a brightness! though I am not enjoying the
first day of spring very much, it is not with me as it is
with my friend George, spending his first spring in the grave:

7

windbaggery, snag-gaggling, yakety-yak, fuss: if you dig
a well, steen it well: earth's fluid: it moves: any
discontinuity imposed, opposing the normal intermingled sway,

must be chocked full of resistance: and with a well, one
can't count on the mechanisms that stay by yielding to the
sway: but if a well, steened well, can stay, it can be

caused to bring together the truly fluid from the so-so:
precise imposition leading to separation, an unmuddling of
clarity, a purification and cleansing invested with identity:

from bunkum and hoarse gol-danging surgical nicety can remove
a truth's modest pleasantry: between the mixtures and
distinctions, what is economy to prefer: a cheap bulk of

8

slush or a costly drop to drink: it is a choice imposition
imposes: for myself I'm tempted to let the well
cave in at times and the water stand to my thirst: I

never did like anything too well done, a scary invitation
to catastrophe: a bright challenge to the insuperable forces:
let it all mosey: there is no final resistance: nor any

endless going along: if nothing in us, under us, or around us
will redeem us, we'd better get used to the miseries: at least,
unbuffaloed about the outcome: well, make the well well or

don't: (it has never occurred to me to face the terror but
as to how to hide from it I'm a virtual booth of information):
come to think of it I don't have much smell in my works:

9

though the surface is crisp with pattern still we know
that there are generalized underlyings, planes of substratum
lessening from differentiation: under all life, fly and

dandelion, protozoan, bushmaster, and ladybird, tendon
and tendril (excluding protocellular organelles) is the same
cell: and under the cell is water, a widely generalized

condition, and under that energy and under that perhaps the
spirit of the place: if we sink we go awash: so
thanks for the surface if also for the deeps: but if we

pass through the discrete downward to the general, may we
not also pass upward, to the high syntheses of overlyings
and radiances, and may it not be so, extremes meeting, that

10

the heights and depths somewhere join in a near-complete
fizzle of the discrete: on either side well-boundaried
by the impassable, our selves float here, as

safely as duration allows, time in its stew mixing as much as
unmixing: I could not say, then, that the earthworm is not
my radical cousin, and I could not say that my veins entering

along the cell walls disresemble the transportative leaf:
I mean, if one speaks of mysticism, it makes good science,
which is the best part of science, that it makes mysticism

discussable without a flurry: and yet, too, the discrete
annihilated, suddenly here it is, blandished and available:
things go away to return, brightened for the passage:

11

desk chair, wheel-back side chair, armchair, country
corner chair, bedside commode, side table, pad-foot
side table, lowboy, credence table, console, drop-leaf

table, writing table, armoire, refectory table, ladder
chair, washstand, pedestal table, tilt-top supper table,
oak coffer, dining chair, settle, bedside table, bureau,

serving table, chest, slant-front bureau, chest-desk,
bureau desk, spindle-back dining chair, kettle table,
corner table, bookcase, chiffonier: in the furniture

of the mind, diversity pushed into distinction is enabling,
a pleasant calculation of possibility: the same can be
said for footwear, glassware, software, and willowware:

12

they say when egalitarianism is legislated into ultimate
ramification, legislation and effect click
heels into totalitarianism: the smoothest sailing's in

a canal, the water as if abstracted out of itself, slack, mere,
unresisting, aerial: while anything you tried to send
down a ravine of boulders would be substantially altered,

even something as compliant, accommodating, as water,
rushed, stirred, whitened, and sprayed, anything more
got-up say a watermelon, likely to be finished: anyone

who knows sharp lakewater or blasted bay water or
open sea water knows where he wants to sail, prizing the
choppy, difficult, and swift: I do not smooth into groups:

13

the shapes nearest shapelessness awe us most, suggest
the god: elemental air in a spin, counterclockwise
for us, lets its needlepoint funnel down and gives us

a rugged variety of the formless formed: and the great
slow stir of the Sargasso cycles the weed in, a holding,
motion's holding: snow from snow kicks up in a fume

and sprinkles audibly the stripped lilac shrubs: the
shape of air, deep as material, blunt off a cliff face: fire
as it crowns out over forests and clings to

itself exploding as if into a new fire: the gods near
their elemental or invisible selves turn or sweep or
stand still and fill us with the terror of apprehending:

14

wood, though, a log, rigid with shape, seems
innocent and meek, accepted, trivial: even starlings,
grazing in a dark patch, move as a bunch, single flights

out or in a small percentage of the potential: the
ashtray sits with a flat, notched containment, powerless:
shape, definition, ease: thank the gods for those

though only the least gods will take them on or those
gods are least who do: but the real gods, why talk
about them, unavailable: they appear in our sight when they

choose and when we think we see them whole, they stall
and vanish or widen out of scope: the highest god
we never meet, essence out of essence, motion without motion:

15

in the generations and becomings of our minds, anthologies,
good sayings are genes, the images, poems, stories
chromosomes and the interminglings of these furnish beginnings

within continuities, continuities within trials, mischances,
fortunate forwardings: gene pool, word hoard: the critic
samples the new thing, he turns it over in his consideration,

he checks alignments, proportions, he looks into the body of
the anthology to see if the new thing hooks in, distorts, to raise
or ruin: he considers the weight, clarity, viability of

the new thing and reconsiders the whole body of the anthology:
if the new thing finds no attachment, if energy, cementing,
does not flow back and forth between it and the anthology,

16

it dies, withered away from the configuration of the people:
but if it lives, critic and teacher show it to the
young, unfold its meaning, fix its roots and extend its reach:

the anthology is the moving, changing definition of the
imaginative life of the people, the repository and source,
genetic: the critic and teacher protect and reveal the source

and watch over the freedom of becomings there: the artist
stands freely into advancings: critic and teacher choose, shape,
and transmit: all three need the widest opening to chance

and possibility, so perceptions that might grow into currents
of mind can find their way: all three are complete men,
centralists and peripheralists who, making, move and stay:

17

groups form—it's natural—agglutinations, a center shaping,
a core center of command and focus: group attaches to group,
some slight delimitation still distingushing them, and region

to region, till a public is formed, however tenuous and
widespread the binding syrup now: my sympathies do not move
that way, building toward the high consolidation (except in

poems), the identifying oneness of populations, peoples: I
know my own—the thrown peripheries, the stragglers, the cheated,
maimed, afflicted (I know their eyes, pain's melting amazement),

the weak, disoriented, the sick, hurt, the castaways, the
needful needless: I know them: I love them: I am theirs:
I can't reach them through the centers of power: the centers

18

of power aim another way from them: I reach them out in the
brush in the rangeful isolation, night: I touch them: I
turn my face into the rock walls and say sayings: the rock

jiggles with magic: the black grass burns darkness, fries:
the brush dances: I do the ones I love no good:
I hold their pain in my hands and toss it in moonlight:

it multiplies and sparkles: I attack trees and wrestle
them to the ground: I roll rocks into heaps and pull the heaps
down: come, I say, with morning, this is the exact specification

of the account: the leg is inflamed: the tooth is aching:
the mind gathers and dissolves, the water is both fast and
deep, the branches are picked clean, but saying is becoming day:

19

oh, it's spring, and I'm more transparent that ever:
I heard the white-breasted nuthatch gurble over the trunk
bark today, and tonight everything is so clear it's

going down to zero: my idealism's as thin as the sprinkled
sky and nearly as expansive: I don't love anybody much:
that accounts for my width and most of my height: but

I love as much as I can and that keeps me here but light:
everything is so plain: death is lake-space, crystal dusk:
(a morning following, the poet still alive but with

a headache, a toothache, a throatache, a jawache, and a
backache, forges on)—though the snow on the lawn has
receded into a numerous archipelago of small valleys and

20

though the boughs on the south side of the blue spruce
hang calm in a heat-holding of the bright sun and though
the garage eave is letting the snow down in a linear rain

still I am not high on the bestseller lists, the Wonderful
Award is gradually being given to someone else (more
deserving) and the money's pouring out: funny, when we

were oriented geocentric (with our heads in the harmonious
skies) we became unsettled by locating vaster centers but
made a rescue by bringing our heads down to a geocentric

identity with the earth, the core-mind of the hot moving
metals, the swimming transitional zone between core and
solidification, and then, of course, the discrete, cool

21

variegated surface: from a large threat, a concise retreat:
a woman in black dress and gray apron spreads mayonnaise
on a slice of bread: the knife glimmers pushing the pliant

ridge before it: there is lettuce but not much light to see
by: maybe ham-and-lettuce-with-mayonnaise (I sometimes
order that): the woman talks softly but urgently to a

heavier woman beside her: they are discussing how the
sandwich is to be made: the procedure is scheduled and, step
by step, must be done right: the dead man who will accompany

the sandwich is either in the next room in a box or right
in the kitchen, which could explain why the women whisper:
he does not yet know he is dead: he wakes underground,

22

feels around for the sandwich: he rises to eat or just
goes back to sleep: or the ham-and-lettuce crackle and
squish in loud teeth and generate light for the eyes: a

new world appears: light that he can move in swells: are
the women done with the sandwich: is it time to tighten
the lid: last-minute placements, arrangements: has the trip

started: I think of the box, the closure underground: I do
not trust the lettuce: eyes of the dead open later in the
dark: I wake: but sail, sail on, oblate spheroid,

feather-light at center, snug about floating dimensions, speed
like a wish in the vacuum, even though for 46 years the
redbird has been red, dropped stones have fallen, beans have

23

twined (counterclockwise, again) up the stakes, merry-go-rounds
have maintained an exhilarating, centrifugal verge: it may
be the mind can wear out the earth: what a put-down

for the enterprising, inventive earth: an empty mind on a
bleached planet: bet on the void: but, of course, nature
sheds deadwood and spins commencements out, tendrils,

surprised to be here and looking forward: a hell of
a way to keep fresh: you could wish nature would accept the
challenge to keep us here and keep us entertained: the mind

has come up with some interestingly inexhaustible quandaries,
at least, nodes resistant, wherein as you go in you come
out, presumably the only stillness a nothingness at the

24

center: a good task for those so minded who would not prefer
to be out regarding waves: bugus ecstaticus: hocus focus:
some things should be forgotten on the grounds that they

aren't worth remembering: coelum empyreum that dries up gods
into luminosities, radiances cooling into sightlessness:
brine, dearth, desolation, sand, the grand circulation, the

lesser circulations trivial, the fireball shrinking and
swelling—bells rung apart from the savagery of a tune, the
word bells of dissonance between the harmonious keys—(play

up the other side a bit, too, some other time), sprite of
falls, now nothing inspires gladness in breaking water: some
things are discrete (who stores gathers thieves) if not

25

dichotomous: but if I back off to take the shape of a tree
I gather blurs: when does water seeping into the roothairs
pass the boundary after which it is tree: the light, the

surrounding, penetrating, shading light, at what aural
remove from the actual leaf does light cease to be tree: or
do the tree boughs linger all the way into the sun: when

the leaves fall, as they are falling now in shoals of variable
intensities, when does the wind have them and the tree give
them up: is the high syrup invisible moving under, through,

and by discretions our true home, not these bodies so much
change makes and ends: but dichotomy, no: I can't divide
structure and function: as one loosens, the other fades:

26

we want to go home and exist in a quietude like merriment
but we can't go home as ourselves but wearing the faces
of many answering things until, faceless, we can't tell we're

home because we are: here in a closing house, we have the
self to have, wherein, however, dreams of home come and go
as with foreigners and exiles: from implacability and

quandary we make shabby or golden peace: pain at the end will
move us like a willing rocket away: short of the cycle of
the natural ongoing is the human, a stream broken, bent,

stalled, re-begun that began back with the first transmissible
molecule and is sticking to time and motion still: if one
adds a point of light to the ongoing mind, one exists with,

27

lodges, a preserved energy, ever able to give energy off,
a great peculiarity, the only immortality known: it is a
real translation but the body dies away from it and even

the species must go by going or changing out of itself:
nothing the biggest subject, total comprehension is
a wipe-out: but if one adds a point of light to ongoing

mind, the point may lock a right angle, righteous with
rigidity, the identity firm but unavailable to accommodation:
but one's point of light may be a worm wriggling away at

a coordinate constant—destructive creativity: it is not
possible to make an altogether favorable decision: the
rightest mind is shadowed by leftovers' dark carriages,

28

the unadducible, the small haunting that tilts
rightmindedness toward the possible: protected from
mental congealing, having finished the pyramid, one recalls

the circle: everything is so clear: the round yew (or
whatever it is) that sits on the lawn like a big green
beachball reacted immediately to coolish weather by

reddening in the berries, and then gangs of cedar waxwings
(maybe it's a cedar) came through and softening up to the
bush, a mellow beating, took the berries, but the softening

is because the bush is, however hard-limbed inside,
peripherally limber, so the birds combine wingy air with
alighting carefully: when they've fed, they can fly off hard

29

and fast: ecstatic as mating, the transforming's pleasing:
a windy dusk, the clouds low and running, the maple leaves
picking up yellow glows, citron pellucidity: spirits

loosen from the ground: unremembered and unresolved are
coming back, breaking free, flapping and gnashing, spooking
the bones of the milling trees, some leaves letting go

skittering streetlight black dances: cats twist frying in
the wind: keep low: the hedges move: there's a lit door:
hello: we're pirates: how can and how long can an identity

hold to the skin of the earth: day before yesterday was
brisk windy, blustery, and a lot of leaves fell, some of
them not quite ready couldn't hold on, and I said if it's

30

calm tomorrow (which was yesterday) not a leaf will fall:
you know the casual fall when a leaf comes off over nothing:
extremity can move ahead of time: but by today others had

mellowed at the pedicel, ready to unclasp to zephyrs: I'm
in touch with spirits: squeaky she-devils, flapping jacks,
batty left-overs: listen: I know Matthew Arnold is not

far off: he's going to come roaring out of the woods, deeply
offended by the briars and limber limbs, and mount up on a
high stone chair and declaim to the woods: he's going to

reinaugurate the distinctions and subordinations that make
sense: he's going to turn the lofty lofty and broad and
force the minuscule into its residence: we're going to climb

31

up the low belly of this sow century, through the seventies,
eighties, right on upward to the attachments, the anterior
or posterior fixation, anything better than the swung pregnancies

of these evil years: considering the fluxions, radiations,
drifts, malleabilities, considering chance and random (what
could be more just than that a united world take its power

from and bring its power to the person—the widest sweep of
unity taking definition and meaning from the unit) (the pheasants
neck-nicking walk out of the snowthickets and explode over

the white paling fence away: it's afternoon, gray, snow:
the eavesdrops a much-intervaled music, alive, unintentioned,
scraggly): considering sensations, rampaging difficulties,

32

poor assessments, it's hard to draw a line, the careful,
arrogant, arbitrary imposition, the divider that blocks off
and sets apart, the arising of difference and distinction:

the discrete a bolus of slowed flux, a locus of depressed
reaction rates, a boned and fibered replication: slowed
but not stopped (heightened within its slows): on the instant

of cessation, disintegration's bacteria flare: bloom, puff,
and blow with change: much energy devoted to staving off
insweeps of alteration: to slow, defer, to chew up change

into the materials of slowing: until the body, increasingly
owed, is paid: take the mind's radiant works, the ground
changes under them: they lift off into distraction: one

33

needs clarities to know what one is baffled by, the small
left- and righthandedness: suppose one saw the nonsupportive
clearly: how could the mind, lit up and possessed, find

energy for salvation's befuddlement: to confront nothingness,
the best baffler, is to disengage monsters and prevent
lofty identifications: to be saved is here, local and mortal:

everything else is a glassworks of flight: a crystal
hankering after the unlikely: futures on the next illusion:
order is the boat we step into for the crossing: when we

step out, nothingness welcomes us: inspiration spends through:
by the snowroad the boulder floats afire: fir-bark,
skittering under a startled squirrel, falls in flames

34

rattling and flecks the burning snow: the moundhill wintered
lean lifts a shackling of cindery trees into the element
unending: the stream, drawing radiance, collects and casts

the light, kindled glancing: mania dries with ash, the
oppressed grows weightless: doze/n th/rough c/and/or man/aged
leg/ions stud/ents: in hill-gold sun, mock orange branches

swim windy shadows, like lean fish in glass, against the
windowpanes: a golden dream swims with the light, schools
of thoughts turning, bunching, heading down, up: nothing is

wrong: all is carrying over: the windowpanes flow with shapes,
fish in a glassen clarity: snowsqualls interrupt but return
the shaking moment: the dream sets off for the sufficient journey:

35

the safety engineers complain that the people are numb
along the fault line and will not survive if they do not
respond to warning signals: maybe so: but how

have we survived at all but by numb nonchalance: to know
and care is to take victory out of the moment when a
moment's victory is what everything is for, apparently:

still, there's no sense in being stupid: floors can
collapse, flopping pancakes, and too much wavering,
even, in the heights can bring files and bookshelves down

on folks: does just a little forethought so diminish the
impulse: must the stadiums, gymnasiums, and grade schools
be put right on the line: still the people know: a

36

few thousand can be spared, but life can't be compromised:
there are so many dangers and possibilities of danger that
even if you entertained them one at a time you'd still be

numb to most of them: but there's no need to be perversely
careless: according to the World Book, the Jabiru wades
the swamps of South America, and the Jaçana's a relative of,

or looks a lot like, the gallinule, of which I, in a recent
unpublished poem, spoke briefly: *I* which suggests *eye*
really derives from a symbol for the hand: and *K* stands

for the palm or open hand: and *J*, you know, is just another
form of *I:* that whole IJK cluster is one of my favorites
in the alphabet, and I specially like the JK vol of the WB:

37

you take me: I never used the word *rink* in my work nor
tosh as in *turgid tosh* nor *slipup, backswing, tocsin,*
discinct, skin-flint, razzmatazz: thank the Lord:

if the world wears out, there are still shenanigans left in
the lingo, more compiled than the world around here which
is mostly winter: but the old quince bush looking like

a mess of last year's baling wire is putting out the redbud
so much that the dry intertwining morning glory vine is
starting to look ridiculous: but those vines outlined so

many beginnings of snow last fall and this spring! and
may yet again so outline the snow, that is, provide a
catchment with configuration no different from the

38

catch itself: most of our writers live in New York City
densely: there in the abstractions of squares and glassy
floors they cut up and parcel out the nothingness they

think America is: I wish they would venture the rural and
see that the woods are undisturbed by their bothering
reputations and that the brooks have taken to flowing

the way they always have and that the redwing pauses
to consider his perch before he lights in a cedar:
I never saw more birds than this cold spring: they are

intervaled foliages to the branchy bushes and trees, so
many comings-in and flyings-out summer and winter mix
in a minute: I don't know their names, leaves that make

39

their own wind of shrieks and whistles: but there's a
bluish small roll of garden wire in the edge of the woods
that shows no sign of sprouting, however naturalized,

the robin striking leaves over by it and staring: leave
it there long enough, it will start to function, a
protective tangle, a harbor or arbor to centipede or

vine, a splinterer of gusts: Apollo 16 just blasted
off: it's 1400 miles downrange at 16,000 mph, orbit
established: a stirring bit of expenditure there in the

blastoff into freefall's silent, floating speed: hurry back,
boys: look out your window at North America: I'm right
under that big cloud: it hasn't budged in six months:

40

John and I drove out to check the paint job on the propjet,
Mohawk merging with Allegheny and losing its emblems and
identifications, such as colors, black and gold, and the

head of the Indian chief on the tail assembly, to the white
and blue streaks, with red lettering, of Allegheny: as
part of his commitment to the baggage man, John stood out

by the wire fence in the pouring rain until the second
engine started to spin and the passenger door went up: then
we stood under a shelter with our hands over our ears while

the plane taxied out on the runway: just then it occurred
to me how much I dislike weekends and how pleasant it would
be to pull Sundays in particular out of the calendar and

41

add a longish month to June: this measure, maw, can grind
up cancers and flourish scarfs of dandelions, manage the
pulp of hung ticks and be the log the stream flows against

for a whole year: its mesh can widen to let everything
breeze through except the invisible: it can float the
heaviest-bloodied scalding dream and sail it into the high

blue loops of possibility: it can comprise the dull
continuum of the omnium-gatherum, wait and wait, without
the alarm of waiting, getting as much being out of motion

as motion out of being: multiple and embracing, sweet
ingestion, the world bloat, extension pushed to the popped
blossoming of space, the taking of due proportion's scope:

42

I think my problems no classier than anyone else's, though:
closure ends all shows, the plain strict and the frowzy
brilliant: and if we go, separately but all together,

to nondistinction, we might as well make as much distinction
here as we can: the proud fall, right, but the great fall
came before, and when one knows he's going out, can we

blame him for shoving the voltage up: I wake in the morning
fairly level with the tide: the dust feels right on my
tongue: but in no time a trifle or two, tardy toaste, ice

on the windshield, the crusty vestments of day, I veer off
into classic compensation, a vision or two shot anger-high,
a little gilded scaffolding toward unreal floors, so I get

43

home at night and go to bed like a show folding: it's
great to get back in the water and feel time's underbuoys,
the cradling saliences of flux, re-accept and rock me off;

then, in nothingness, sinking and rising with everyone not
up late: the plenitude: it's because I don't want some
thing that I go for everything: all the people asleep with

me in sleep, melted down, mindlessly interchangeable,
resting with a hugeness of whales dozing: dreams nudge us
into zinnias, tiger lilies, heavy roses, sea gardens of

hysteria, as sure of sunlight as if we'd been painted by
it, to it: let's get huzzy dawn tangleless out of bed,
get into separateness and come together one to one: you

44

who are showless and self-full, be generous, come by, offer
me a chat: I'd trade my shows in any day for the real thing:
meanwhile, amusement, a waiting amusement, is my study—I

hope you will take it at no other level: this measure moves
to attract and hold attention: when one is not holding one,
that is a way of holding: dip in anywhere, go on until the

attractions fail: I angle for the self in you that can be
held, had in a thorough understanding: not to persuade you,
enlighten you, not necessarily to delight you, but to hold

you: the lofty, shot high by constraint, adopt the rigor
of scary levitation, grow icy by the swirl of fear as much
as by the vacant, sizable view, but sometimes imagine they

45

are flying: but the mirrorments, astonishments of mind,
what are they to the natural phenomena, the gross destructions
that give life, we cooling here and growing on a far outswing

of the galaxy, the soaring, roaring sun in its thin-cool
texture allowing us, the moon vacant though visitable, Mars
not large enough to hold an air, Venus too hot, so much

extravagance of waste, how can the bluegreen earth look
purposeful, turn a noticeable margin to meaning: what are
mirrorments, then, so shatterable, liable to melt, too

much light, the greasy graying of too much time: man waited
75,000 years in a single cave (cold, hunger, inexplicable
visitation of disease) only to rise to the bright, complex

46

knowledge of his destruction! that heaviness weighs down,
lacking an interpenetrating spiritual float: but were men,
starting out three million years ago, calling up to us:

if they were not able to call up to us, what was in them able
to call them up: what was the hidden, interior elixir that
glided them along the ground, gave them the speech of staring

into their dumfounded hands: or did they turn in each day's
light, storming the world for food and place, merely and
sufficiently: when we have made the sufficient mirror will

it have been only to show how things will break: know thyself
and vanish! and the knowledge not for itself or the self
but so the ambience may call itself vacantly expressed,

47

fully exfoliated, empty! sunrise this morning was not
a fraction: it was self-full, whole in motion: the man
falling asleep in the cave winters of time ago swayed

into the fullness, assumed the measure: we are as in a
cone of ages: each of us stands in the peak and center
of perception: around us, in the immediate area of recent

events, the planets make quickly-delivered news and the sun
acquaints us of its plumes eight minutes old: but then
the base widens dropping back and down in time through

the spinal stars of spirals and deepens broadening into
the core of our configuration with its ghostly other side:
and then the gulfs and deepenings begin and fall away

48

through glassy darkness and shadowy mind: antiquity on
antiquity the removes unveil, galaxies neighbors and foreign
cousins and groups of galaxies into the hazy breadths and

depths the telescope spells its eye to trace: but here
what took its beginning in the farthest periphery of event,
perception catches the impact of and halts to immediacy,

the billion-year-old flint light striking chemical changes
into the eye: behold: the times break across one
another like waves in surfy shoals and explode into the

white water of instantaneous being: each of us stands in
the cone of ages to collect the moment that breaks the
deeper future's past through: each of us peak and center:

49

who owns nothing has everything and who owns something
has that: snow's a reservoir spring springs with leaks,
interminglings of onrush and withholding: how close *middle*

comes to the middle of the dictionary: make a mighty
force, that of a god: endow it with will, personality, whim:
then, please it, it can lend power to you: but then you

have created the possibility of its displeasure: what you
made to be greater than you is and enslaves you and then
suppose trying to be free again you begin upward desperate

identifications until those identifications enlarge beyond
you and terrify you and move you out of the frame of actual
gestures: take my advice: the forces are there all right

50

and mostly beyond us but if we must be swayed by the forces
then at least let's be the only personalities around, the
sort of greatness a raft in a rapids is and at the top

let's put nothingness, good old: the most open suasion:
a darkness in the method, a puzzling, obfuscating surface,
is the quick (and easy) declaration of mystery, with the risk,

though, that should the method come plain, be made out, the
mystery, surficial, its elements jumbled, would disappear,
unless, of course, under the quick establishment of difficult

method the true mystery survived: it's not necessarily true
that things left to themselves go to pieces: without the help
of human hand, for example, far from the scaffolding of the

51

human imagination, old (presumed) Chaos stirred in himself,
spirals (cellular whirlwinds), upward swoops of bending aspiration,
collisions high with potentials of linkage, dissolvings and

meldings lengthy and free—these "motions" brought particles
into progression often: if the progressions often failed into
tatterdemalions, do-funnies, whatchamacallits, and thingumbobs,

there was time enough in the slow motions of landforms, oceans,
of moon and sun for Chaos to undo and recommence: certain
weaves caught on to random hooks and came into separation and

identity: and found ways to cause the causes of origin to
recur with increasing frequency: one must be careful not to bestow
intention where there may have been no more (much) than jostling

52

possibility: keep jiggling the innumerable elements and
even integrations can fall out of disintegrations: in any case,
physicochemical phenomena account sufficiently for the

output up to now: but all movements are religious: inside
where motions making up and rising turn about and proceed,
node and come to pass, prayer is the working in the currents,

hallelujahs dive and sculp the mud, mazes of mud melting away
from the slurpy lifting loads: when the mob goes wild and thrashes
a bit copulating, shaking the bushes, it is moving in service:

when one screams in terror of the Most High, he is asserting
his hunger for the merely usual and mortal, for the circum-
scription of place: the polar bear snarling or running,

53

diving or sleeping, attunes to the accuracy of the imperative:
sketchiness and incompleteness, broken gestures, stuttering
intentions, fact blanching and breaking fiction, seizures

of cold and pied heat, these are prayerful realizations of
disorientation, holy efforts to accept or change: nothing,
not even the least (the half-step or stalled intention) is

without the rigor of knowing: how to be saved: what is
saving: come to know the motions with what rightness, accuracy,
economy, precision they move and identify the motions of the

soul with them so as to find the self responsive to and in
harmony with the body of motions: morality is not a judgment
on action but acting rightly, truly—total, open

54

functioning: how to make the essential fashionable is the
problem without promoting boredom for there is little variation
day to day in the essential and, worse, when the fashionable

hangs on it loses the quality of the fashionable: of course
we are sure that the fashionable relates only peripherally
to the essential so that it is nearly certain that to be

fashionable is not to be essential: there is the aspect,
though, of change that it is constant so that always to be
fashionable is to participate in the lasting: problems

problems: the essential without specification is boring
and specification without the essential is: both ways out
leaves us divided but so does neither way: unless—and here

55

is the whole possibility—both essential and fashionable can
be surrounded in a specified radial essential, which is difficult:
imagining withered conditions (for company), I think of

settled bulk, the ancient bristlecone, a sprout surviving
fanny: down South there: when they want to say *magnificent* they
say most-maggie-went-a-fishing: does'em good: have atchoo

and a couple of belches: when I was a freckle-faced boy, said
they warn't no freckles but fart bran from following cows:
said I was a redheaded woodpecker: I was redheaded: I been

humiliated: now, I'm a redheaded, woody pecker: stand
up, stand up for beauty, thou soldier of the breechjammed hole,
garrison gates, thou wayfarer upon the breastworks and

56

ramparts (ram parts), thou regular maker of meter, convivial iamb,
sleuthy sluice: halt, hut, two: what we believe in requires no
believing: if the axe falls on the toe, severance will

follow promptly: put the burner on Hi the coffee will boil:
push down the fence it will no longer be standing: walk off
the cliff, air greets you: so much we do not need to

be urged to believe, we're true, true believers with no
expenditure of will: to believe what runs against the
evidence requires belief—concentration, imagination, stubbornness,

art, and some magic: the need to disbelieve belief so disbelief
can be believed: there are infidels only of fictions: not
a single temple has been raised to the fact that what is raised

57

falls, yet that is the lesson: here's my credo: if the merry-
go-round goes too fast it will be difficult to hold on: if you
pull up the rosestock, you lose your hips: certitude plus:

everything in moderation including moderation: when you come
to know the eternal forces realizing themselves through form
you will need to lay on no special determination to assent

to what demands none: but if truth is colorless, fictions
need be supreme, real supreme with hot-shot convincingness
and lashes laid on lavishly for the doubter, and, per

usual, regular dues: gentlemen of the naked vision, let us
see straight: here we are today and here we are not tomorrow:
if you kick the sand you are likely to raise some dust:

58

if you bite me in the ear, I will knee you in the nuts:
if you do something nice for me, I will feel encouraged to do
something nice for you: fight on my side, we fight together:

aleatory composition and choral improvisation throwback to
dinosaur lagoons, the much floating, winged sawbills,
bankless, ambient figurings, dismemberments of breath by

overhanging fern-spun ramification: I hear the swirls of
morays, I think, breathing undersea, and see shadows
of mantas remora travel in: but which way is this distant—

a throwback or coming: I'm aware of the military-industrial
complex and of lust for erosion: I hear in choral breakings
in and out clamoring gulls guzzling a clam shoal washed up

59

rank: I hear us coming to a pass and just beyond the ridge
sawbills chirr circling an outbreak of undamageable light:
a single dot of light, traveling, will memorize the sphere:

redemptions despise the reality: when may it not be our
task so to come into the knowledge of the reality as to
participate therein: wherever the imagined lands it's

likely to brush up against a thorn and pop or get hit by
a bus on the freeway or at the minimum be thought flatulent:
I wonder where all on what ledges, on what nordic heights

or high sinkages of meadow the aspen grows and where all
popular breaks out in shivering testimonial under bright skies,
if along irrigation ditches, flat lengths into diminishment,

60

regimentation of strict discipline, or at the edges of backwoods
fields, off from the sight of anything save night's night bird or
day's night bird: I wonder where all seagulls follow the plow,

how far inland, or float serene in dislocation on sweetwater
lakes, I wonder where all along the bottoms of what hills the
roses open their brief and failing rages: ardency is a

calf, butting and guzzling, let free to the cow: a luminous
saint reeling in the heights of objectless desire: hornets
after rain splitting out for lit flies: my heart shakes,

my eyes concentration's flames, you my attention, absolute:
dust travels, gets up into the wind's limbs and through
stirrings and catchments makes itself available to new

61

coherences, settles out, for example, carrying in microscopic
branches paramecium, virus, germ to damp stayings,
boom bloomings, gets going to return: leaves nothing lost:

the field widens—at the same time the essential begins
to take shape: an immense victory unfolds before me: my
potassium-laced diet (jiggers of orange juice) will free me

from episodes of irregular heartbeats, premature ventriculations,
and the misimpressions ads for nonprescription painkillers
pain me with: I expect to promote good will and difficult

clarities: I'm tired of bumfuzzlement and bafflement: and
I expect to give my friends who have found it impossible to
love me grounds for further trials: a big clinkery is a big

62

cinder field or a clinkery of big cinders: a fish out of water's
out for water: grief is all I know and joy all I understand:
news item—search of creek nets no new results: today's

radicalism is tomorrow's triviality: but excellence,
one of the forming principles of the universe, is ever
radical: garrulity is harm enough even when, as here, it

finds harmless way: but novelty, like garrulity, is one
of the forming principles, so much waste and ill-conceiving
before invention provides advancement to the ongoing:

for a form to complete everything with! orb: but this is the
procedure: if everything's put in, the boundary bursts and
one is nowhere except picking up havoc's fragments, things

63

nowise as shapely in their selfness as before: but
settling in the beginning for fency definition, that straight
reach across the variable field, chokes the pulse, bores

the tame, excludes the free rush of imagination except as
wind or as a small consistency like sand: the only bearable
fence is the continuum, the scope of oneness under which

the proud ephemerals play discretely in their energizing
laws and play out, transformations taking their ways, bending
their boundaries, giving and losing: the outface of the

sphere, the skinny seat on infinity, this holding, this
gentle stay in the bosom of reconciling but progressing
motions: the universes, they say, warp, bend, plunge into

64

dark centers that blossom white into other spaces, but in
the slope and backwater of some ancient events, the meld
cools into solidifications, white roots lift green leafages,

mold blooms pink and orange in the shade, and maggots race
like traveling waves in the stems of brief, huge mushrooms:
in this open form there's room enough for everything to find

its running self-concisions and expansions, its way, its
definition, down to the precious least: (when an image or
item is raised into class representative of cluster, clump,

or set, its boundaries are overinvested, the supercharge is
explosive, so that the burden of energy overwhelms the matter,
and aura, glow, or spirituality results, a kind of pitchblende,

65

radium, sun-like: and when the item is moved beyond class
into symbol or paradigmatic item, matter is a mere seed
afloat in radiance: it is the mystery, if reasonable, that

when the one item stands for all, the one item is so lost
in its charge that it is no longer bounded but all radiance:
this is the source of spirit, probably, the simple result of

the categorizing mind: the mind will forever work in this way,
and the spiritual, the divine, always be with us: in the
comprehensiveness and focus of the Most High is the obliteration

total that contains all and in that we rest, moving as we like
back into change and boundary and back: since these procedures
will not change, we may think rescue omnipresent, a calming,

66

and may exist in that really through the last change: a state
of mind can override the worst tendency and not, even in
surrender to the tendency, be false to its state: to live in

the shifts of facts, unorganized and dark, is to know only
generation, mindless, fallen, senselessly repeating: things
work in these ways: deliverance a way they allow): what,

April 23rd and still not a daffodil: suddenly as if a
bright bird had passed, one is old: one dozes forgetful of what
one was for: a suspension of interrelationships: the reader is

the medium by which one work of art judges another: hypnosis
is induced by focusing the attention: the trinket swings
or spins before the eyes, the normal flood of distractions

67

that keeps one awake is drained, and the mind sinks into
simplified ease: the poem, its rhythm, is exclusive and hypnotic,
too, but the poem keeps enough revelant variety going to interest

the mind from sleep but enough focus to disinterest it in
external matters: a hypnotic focus, then, that is awakening,
a focus of controlled fullness, not over-exclusiveness: but

the purpose of the motion of a poem is to bring the focused,
awakened mind to no-motion, to a still contemplation of the
whole motion, all the motions, of the poem: this is very

different from hypnosis: a descent into the subconscious
(tentacles maybe into the unconscious) is prepared for not by
blotting out the conscious mind but by intensifying the alertness

68

of the conscious mind even while it permits itself to sink,
to be lowered down the ladder of structured motions to the
refreshing energies of the deeper self: but why is it of use

to be brought through organized motion from chaos and
ephemerality to no-motion: to touch the knowledge that
motions are instances of order and direction occurring

briefly in the stillness that surrounds: to touch, to know,
to be measured and criticized by the silence, to acknowledge
and surrender to wholeness and composure: the non-verbal

energy at that moment released, transformed back through the
verbal, the sayable poem: spirit-being, great one in the world
beyond sense, how do you fare and how may we fare to Thee:

69

people set out to serve the people become those the people
serve: given the skinny poles of fact to theory, person to
man, event to continuum, how are we to develop intermediacy:

what is to be done, what is saving: is it so to come to know
the works of the Most High as to assent to them and be reconciled
by them, so to hold those works in our imaginations as to think

them our correspondent invention, our best design within the
governing possibilities: so to take on the Reason of the Most
High as to in some part celebrate Him and offer Him not our

flight but our cordiality and gratitude: so to look to the
moment of consciousness as to find there, beyond all the
individual costs and horrors, perplexing pains and seizures,

70

joy's surviving radiance: I ask because I am terrified of my
arrogance and do not know and do not know if the point in the
mind can be established to last beyond the falling away

of the world and the dreams of the world: but if we are small
can we be great by going away from the Most High into our own
makings, thus despising what He has given: or can we, accepting

our smallness, bend to cherish the greatness that rolls through
our sharp days, that spends us on its measureless currents: and
so, for a moment, if only for a moment, participate in those means

that provide the brief bloom in the eternal presence: is this
our saving: is this our perishable thought that imperishably
bears us through the final loss: then sufficient thanks for that:

71

there is a faculty or knack, smallish, in the mind that can turn
as with tooling irons immediacy into bends of concision, shapes
struck with airs to keep so that one grows unable to believe that

the piling up of figurements and entanglements could proceed from
the tiny working of the small, if persistent, faculty: as if the
world could be brought to flow by and take the bent of

that single bend: and immediately flip over into the mirrored world
of permanence, another place trans-shaped with knackery: a brook in
the mind that will eventually glitter away the seas: and yet pile

them all up, every drop recollected: a little mill that changes
everything, not from its shape, but from change: the faculty
then can be itself, small, but masterful in the face of size and

72

spectacular ramification into diversity: (the way to have a following
is to get up in front of whatever is moving and start waving your
arms): (sir, the piece you have sent me on poetic process and

psychotherapy errs not in being wrong but in being rudimentary: the
poetic consciousness beginning at a center works itself out by
incorporation until through craft, experience, insight, etc., it

brushes in a fulsome way against the fulsomeness of nature so that
on the periphery it is so deeply spelt out that it can tangle with
the coincidental: this provides a growing edge to change and surprise

so that unexpectedness is constantly being fed into the engines of
assimilation and probability, giving shades of tone and air
to the probabilities that make them mean slightly adjusted things):

73

if raindrops are words, the poet is the cloud whose
gathering and withholding overspills generously and unmissed
from a great keeping: (depression, low pressure area): the

false poet is a white wisp that tries to wrest itself into
a storm: but the true storm moseys on with easy destructions
like afterthoughts: how else but by greatness can the huge

presence exist between the gifty showers, twists and blow-outs:
on the way back from Northfield today (April 29, I've been
away a few days to Baltimore) I wrote a poem as follows:

when I go up into the mountains, I like to go up into the
mountains: when I come down from the mountains, I like to
come down from the mountains: there has to be something ahead

74

to like: it might as well be what is ahead: I found this
word *repodepo* in the newspaper only to find it, apparently,
a mischance of machinery: I could not myself have invented

a nonexistence so probable, insignificance so well made: let
it stand for a made nothing, a pointer with no point: or
for anything about which the meaning is insecure: a heavy

registration: a cluster of empty pods, or a special phonetic
depot, or something that repods pseudopods: a leaf cannot
appear on or fall from the branch except via the total

involvement of the universe: you and I cannot walk the street
or rise to the occasion except via the sum total of effect
and possibility of the universe: we are not half-in and

75

half-out of the universe but unmendably integral: when we
move, something yields to us and accepts our steps: our
tensions play against, find rightness in, other tensions not

our own: we move into the motions with our tiny oars: there
are seas not oceans but invisible seas: they sustain,
they drown, but the abundance, the intricacy and dispersion,

is glorious: hope lends silverness to that edge: having
been chastened to the irreducible, I have found the
irreducible bountiful: the daffodil nods to spring's zephyr:

when the grackle's flight shadows a streak of lawn, constellations
of possibility break out, for example, the multitude of
grassblade shadows subsumed in a sweep: for example, an aphid

76

resting in bugleleaf shade must think lost his discretion of
position: (his feelers notice, his eyes adjust): an ant
struck by the flashed alteration stops, the friction of which

event gives off a plume of heat, a small invisible boom:
myriad chloroplasts circling the cell peripheries kick out
of photosynthetic gear and coast in a slough and many atoms

of carbon and nitrogen miss connection: if you dyed the grass
at day's end, you'd see a white streak of starchless loss:
thermodynamics is inscrutable here: the coolant wings, heat

currents, wind currents fanned into unpredictable motions:
when an immense afternoon darkbottomed thunderhead hoves rearing
over the ridge, you can imagine how unencompassing and flustered

77

I get—night a full coming uninterrupted into difference: at
clarity of zooming, I'm unpassed in Cayuga Heights, unparalleled
(nobody hanging on that wing, baby) possibly: at easing

into orbit grease, nuzzling right in there with not a touch
till the whole seal smacks: at that I'm unusually salient,
gritless in curvature with withal enthralling control,

perfection of adjustment, innocence of improvisation beginners
and old strumpets of the spirit know: I don't want shape:
I'll have water muscles bending streams (recurrences of

curvature): wind sheets erect, traveling: lips accommodating
muscle glides: identity in me's a black, clear bead: I've
strongboxed and sunk it, musseled and barnacled with locks,

78

but it's breathing in there, a dumb eager little botch: I aim
absolutes at it so blasting, recoil and strike unnerve my
stability: (from so small a thing, what distant orbits I've

taken into residence) but it's not now form against that form:
it's motion: the renunciation of boxes, magicless: I'll
put the speck in soak, dissolve it, or pump fluids in so dense

flooding will work it out: what is its nature that has caused
so many engines, some fearful: I do not think bat or rat:
it's a sprout child: it coos: it coos pink: the world and I

oppose it: it mustn't see light as itself: it must appear
dissolved, transfigured, or go down with the body it meant to
bloom into the various distractions of decay: then the little

79

breath will die: then the locks, so many, will cast: to
that late funeral of my true self, no weeper will come,
hushing attendant, twelve-footed accompanist: then the small

self will taste the ruin that has been my only food: (one
whose home is afire wanders): just now it's 7:15 and
thunderstormy, blue deepened evening green, somewhat windy,

rain a likely solution: (when ground trash blooms all ways
at once like a flower, something has descended): though I
have a bunch of potential any mush of which could sharpen

into cutting blooms, I sometimes lose definition tendencies
by looking out: look out: the tiny invites attention:
outward concentrations: (the poem reaches a stillness

80

which is its form): crush a bug and the universe goes hollow
with hereafter: in the cemeteries a shiver settles: sparrows
played down to speech in the cedar bunch into flowers:

across the valley a one-sided rim rises, highways like
caterpillars climb to the biting edge: the wings of red-ant
queens clamp flat macadam pools, the queens free-climbing

mirrored trees to the extinction of overhead boughs: fear's
a reservoir inscrutable rivers feed: I'm at the dammed
gate sizzling utterance: spending fear into any shape that

can manage the investment: cypress, weed, swallow-drink,
serpent-drink: to the huge air's multiple fuzzy tongues
I address vague hosannas: evaporation without arithmetic of

81

loss: what a blessing: I have too much to weigh, shape
into meaningful expenditure: I need jars, jugs, hogsheads,
vials: here's a drop to pierce your ear for: have a large

pendant with lesser spangles: send folks over: I have
plenty to pass around: the right investment's in decay,
decayable: brothers, fine brothers, be strong, be merry:

girls, she falcons, be thin: let us work ourselves asleep
against you: you are rocks that bend and flow, take in our
nervous edges: be the blossoms we spend into flower: I go

on the confidence that in this whole magnificence nothing is
important, why should this be, yet everything is, even this
as it testifies to the changing and staying: as man, singular

82

in certain kinds of feeling (we don't know what shades of
feeling travel the weed) I know importances, love, grief,
terror, that can retire nature into strangeness, but until

I get right enough to appreciate the lesser celandine by
the woodsroad, I have not achieved the calm necessary to the
joys of small riches, the briar bud bending out into the path:

feelings, feelings: conceptualization nowhere nears so accurate
a source: nevertheless, except within the highrising dome,
canopy, reach of the forming intellect, feeling has no meaning,

no guidance, but stir, rush, the splintering cycles of small
beginnings and endings, the *sui generations* of particularity:
New York City can be grown over by birch brush: south of

83

Scranton, birch has covered the slag and shale heaps (terrains
of conical spills), the crevices catching dust and leaves,
roots and ice granulating edges: it will be lovely someday,

if left alone, and have a brook: I feel like a brook shedding
a hill, the glassy wide and the thick white falling, a
scud-cover of moss, with a copse here and there of something

quailing, pine in a catchment moved high, a bear's cold red
tongue sloshing in a runlet, and a deer's eye shot with flight:
I am there pondering berries and the bear: my mind furnishes

a clear sky and smart wind: for me, there's more death behind
than ahead, though ahead lies the finish endless: the
seventeen-year-old self is gone and with it the well and

84

wellsweep, chinaberry tree, the mother and father, the two
sisters, living but lost back there, and Silver, Doll, all
the jonquils, the smokehouse, mulberry tree, but when I was

last by, the pecan tree's still standing, the same one, big,
the lean growths and lean shades vanished: more death done
than to do, except that memory grows, accumulating strata of

change, and the eyes close on a plenitude, suddenly, directly
into nothingness: so, in a sense, there's more and more to do
with increasing reluctance: a world if not the world:

I am standing by the hill brook with the hill wife: but
where did all the mosquitoes come from: I'm tired of raw
nuts and berries and staying up late freezing with no

85

television: you can't keep visions selective enough: they
fill up with reality, too gravid grown to keep off the ground:
as we return to the dust from which we came, the gods die

away into the sky, the womb of gods: from the common
universalized materials we ascend into time and shape, hold our
outlines and integrations a while, then stiffen with the

accumulations of process, our bodies filters that collect
dross from the passages of air and water and food, and begin
to slow, crack, splinter, and burst: the gods from the high wide

potentials of aura, of encompassing nothingness, flash into
concentration and descend, taking on matter and shape, color,
until they walk with us, but divine, having drawn down with them

86

the reservoirs of the skies: in time the restlessness that is in
them, the overinvestment, casts the shells of earth to remain with
earth, and the real force of the gods returns to its heights

where it dwells, its everlasting home: these are the mechanics
by which such matters carry out their awesome transactions:
if the gods have gone away, only the foolish think them gone

for good: only certain temporal guises have been shaken
away from their confinements among us: they will return, quick
appearances in the material, and shine our eyes blind with adoration

and astonish us with fear: the mechanics of this have to do with
the way our minds work, the concrete, the overinvested concrete,
the symbol, the seedless radiance, the giving up into meaninglessness

87

and the return of meaning: but the gods have come and gone
(or we have made them come and go) so long among us that
they have communicated something of the sky to us making us

feel that at the division of the roads our true way, too,
is to the sky where with unborn gods we may know no
further death and need no further visitations: what may have

changed is that in the future we can have the force to keep
the changes secular: the one: many problem, set theory, and
symbolic signifier, the pyramid, the pantheon (of gods and

men), the pecking order, baboon troop, old man of the tribe,
the hierarchy of family, hamlet, military, church, corporation,
civil service, of wealth, talent—everywhere the scramble for

88

place, power, privilege, safety, honor, the representative
notch above the undistinguished numbers: second is as good
as last: pyramidal hierarchies and solitary persons: the

hierarchies having to do with knowledge and law, the solitaries
with magic, conjuration, enchantment: the loser or apostate
turns on the structure and melts it with vision, with

summoning, clean, verbal burning: or the man at the top may
turn the hierarchy down and walk off in a private direction:
meanwhile, back at the hierarchy, the chippers and filers

hone rocks to skid together: the bottom rocks have much to
bear: the next level, if buoyed up from below, hardly less:
but the top rock, however nearly in significant flotation,

89

is responsible for the symmetry of the whole, the office of
highsounding purpose, noble gesture, pulling together (by
which is meant pressing up though of course it's pressing

down—but everyone below is willing to bear some weight if
it feels uplifting): the manager's office is 14 x 20 and
the vice president's 16 x 20 and the executive vice president's

18 x 20 and the president's 20 x 20 and the chairman of the board's
the golf course or private jet: for identity and/or effect,
exclude the extraneous, which, though, leaves the identity

skimpy and the effect slight: great procedures move the
other way, inclusively, but with the hold back that when they
have everything they have nothing, an all-ness of identity

90

and no effect, a calm, resolved effect: you can't win: you
can strike balances and, for laughter or sublimity, imbalances
enough to keep the show going, but even at the midpoint of

perfect balances you can suspend oppositions which are no more
than self-cancellations: all identities and effects are
imbalances: but then you get into balancing imbalances,

the effect of most narrative: force mind from boxes to radiality:
the maple buds open into a basket of spangles, a vased bouquet:
greenish-yellow five-petaled flowers, not noticeable or attractive:

I wonder if maples depend on bees: I haven't seen bee one: pulled
the old lawnmower out of the garage after a long winter and it
started right up, two good tugs on the spinning rope: cut the grass,

91

first time of the year: real green grass: been raining so much
people can't get to mowing and then when they do lawnmower chokes
up with blackgreen chunks and clumps, muffling the blade and stalling

the motor: yesterday (May 6) we drove up to Phil Booth's house
and there he was: his wife, Margaret, too, his youngest daughter,
three dogs (all different kinds) and one cat: what a great day: he

cooked outdoor hamburgers and hotdogs: he has fossils in his rocks:
George (P.E.) was there, good old George, and Mary Emma: and
others
all come to the picnic: a brook runs right through Philip's

yard and falls over rocks, gets up and goes on: you can
stand on the rocks and not fall off in the water: the youngest
dog runs around and looks up at you as if wondering what

92

is so surprising: intense and quizzical: I wonder why dogs
haven't learned more in all these years: they take the proper
attitude: what is true service: the true question: or of

the many services, which ones are most nearly true: it
must be a service that is celebration, for we would celebrate
even if we do not know what or how, and for He is bountiful if

slow to protect and recalcitrant to keep: what we can celebrate
is the condition we are in, or we can renounce the condition
we are in and celebrate a condition we might be in or ought

to be in: should we like the saint, ascetic, or priest spurn
the world, sensuous and sensual, and celebrate those longings
in us, sweet heights, that seem the potential of a necessary

93

coming: or should we fall to the pleasures and raggednesses
so relentlessly and opulently provided here, the flappings of
the flesh, the ghostly agonies, the long bleak streaks, commitment

to love's threshing flesh brings on: do we celebrate
most truly when we fall into our limitations, accept our
nothingness of years, spawn, beget, care for, weep, fail, burn,

slobber, suck, stroke, dream, shake, sleep, eat, swim, squirm:
does He forgive us, does he accept our celebration, when we turn
away from the fruits given and hunger after Him—the

arrogance!—His silver and immortal agencies: will He not afflict
us with loss of life in life with nothing later of another kind:
when we take the needy hand in hand, when the tear humbles

94

us with horrible splendor, when tenderness is fully placed
in the human eye, we find service exceeding body into sky:
when anxiety rises words too start to stir rising into schools,

moving into sayings (a recourse, though delusional) like winds
making up before a mild May-evening thunderstorm, the winds
spilling across the trees, then like surf sucking back in a

growing tug: at such times, I pick up a tape, stick the end
into my typewriter, and give everything a course, mostly
because in a storm course is crucial and in proportion to the

storm must be fought for, insisted on: I've weathered a batch
of storms: the words rising from behind the palings of
the back fence, getting loose and showering up from the points

95

of maple leaves, shaking loose in wind-defined drifts
of elm seed, take on configuration of motion and spiel
out into spelling: the few drops of rain have put a fizz

on the street and the cars go by in splitting noticeability:
I just finished planting the pole beans, the zucchini and
cucumbers and transplanted the pepper plants, asters, and

petunias: I had the best time: and after the first shower,
the catbird lit on the top bar of the jungle gym and ripped
off a few bars, as if a surprise announcement: but I know

where that bird's nest is and how quiet it's been around
there this month: I like to think the bird just went
out of his mind with all the rising and fell afloat of it

96

with a singing: that's the way I do it when I do, and I
know the bird's meaning at least in coming to my own: all
the greens, a company of differences, radiant, the source

sunk, the mellowing left-over light suffusing: I thought
I saw a piece of red paper in the grass but it was a
cardinal: and I thought I saw a clump of quince blossoms

move but that was a cardinal: one morning three orioles
were in the green-red quince bush: that was what it was:
the pear tree looks like lime sherbet with whipped cream

topping: the bottom part all leaves and no blossoms and
the top part all blossoms and no leaves: a green sailboat
or a spring mountain, from tree-green to conic, glacial white:

97

the work of the staying mind is to burn up or dissolve the day's
images, the surface falling of pear petals or of hailstones
from the blue bottoms of thunderheads at sea, the curling up and

vanishing or the plopping and melting: for the mind, large as its
surface is, hasn't room for the spreading out of each day's
images to the hard edges: so the subterranean fires of the mind

float upward into the day's business and here and there like
volcanoes burn through into dream meldings, the hard
edges turning inward then moving out assuming their own

foliages and lineations, essentialized: the white hot mouth spewing
up islands recovered to the conscious mind: in this way all the
sensory bits are made available in symbolical assimilations ready to

98

train the mind through its surprises and commonplaces: I am
waiting for the evening star to appear in the windowpane but
the sun's still a ruddy burnishing fire in the lower branches of the

tamarack: this afternoon I thought Jove had come to get me: I walked
into a corridor of sunlight swimming showering with turning shoals
of drift pollen and not yet knowing it was pollen thought perhaps I

was being taken or beamed aboard but saw over the roof the high swags
of the blue spruce swaying and felt stabilized from wonder:
I would still rather beget (though I can't, apparently) than be

begotten upon, I think I'm almost sure, but I don't know that a vague
coming of a shimmery gold floating would be so bad: I sneezed: my
eyes watered: the intimacy was sufficient: nothing is separate:

99

there's the evening star and two jets blazing sunlit vapor trails:
stentorian: tendentious: sonorous: orotund: the moon's up:
however provisional the procedure, tentative the thought, the

days clang shut with bronze finality: days wherein we wavered
studiously with uncertainty, went this way a way and that way a
way, thought twice, take on the hard and fast aspect of the

finished, the concluded fact, thus misrepresenting us: and then
there is at the end the stone that makes it all look purposeful
and deliberate, what was hesitation, gaping, and wondrous

turning around: life takes on the cast of decision and seeds
the ground with marmoreal memento: stone outcroppings in the
pasture like sheep resting: I'm glad the emphasis these days

100

is off dying beautifully and more on a light-minded living with
the real things—soap, spray-ons, soda, paper towels, etc.—for
indelicacy taints taking oneself too seriously and saving life

up to close with a serene finish: I expect to die in terror:
my mother did: old songs (hymns) erupted from her dying
imaginations: they say she sang them blurred for two nights

before the interval of clearing that preceded her majestic
drawing away: my father's heart burst finally and he coasted
off, a cool drifting out of course: these destinations we

think we do not wish to attain: unsettling flurries and
disconnections, hurries and worries, strictures and
besiegings like preparations for camping out: driven, I go

101

into high and drive as fast as I can: driving faster than
I'm driven I can keep the forces aligned and taut but if
a holiday comes along and I try to slow down for vacation,

I swerve a lot, meander and hassle, my driver drives over
my driving, an overdrive taken over by overtaking, hopeless,
hapless helplessness: better trim the quince bush now before

the thorns of new growth harden: or come fall there'll be a
further periphery-thicket of spines: maybe one isn't supposed
to trim while the shoots are still purplish and tender:

doing it now may bleed and depress the bush to death: but
meanwhile, while doing it, I find the placid quince rage
enticing: by now the old periphery of blossom and nub-green

102

quince is inward in an exceeded stratum: even though the bush
has put on the strain of blossoming and fruiting, it has
at the same time shot out shoots all over, threatening the

upcoming hollyhock and lemon lilies: a green rage to possess,
make and take room: to dominate, shade out, whiten: I
identify with the bush's rage, its quiet, ruthless, outward

thrust: whatever nears me must shrink, wither up, or widen
overlarge and thin with shade, ambition the size of the room
I need to unfold into: but cunning and deviousness are at

work at the quince bush: morning glory stock is underground,
ready to shoot up a spear of leaving through the quince's
underbrush and by fast moving to overcrown the bush tops

103

and take the light away: look at the smooth-cut lawn, how
even and gentle: but finger through the turf, the nap,
and there are the brown twists of clover, veronica, plantain,

grass in a striving: it is hard to stand up crowding full
into a full unfolding: being's terror: I wonder if we
should pick the gems out of the reliquary crowns and

give to the poor, boons and munificences showering, plenty
of meat, wines medicinal, soothing beer, classic pretzels:
I wonder if we should shave the gold from the gold reliquary

beards and cast it to flurries of gleaning: or melt down
the artful forms, float off the dross, and mold the gold
or stamp it into guinea suns: then the poor could have

104

their operations, pay off their loans, and thrive with comfort:
the babies could get fresh milk and the lovers could propose:
(but if we demolish the past's imposing achievements, hold

away only the lyre upon which we can plink immediacy): scared
sacred: how dark it gets before the hail starts! lightning
fries in quick crisps, thunder splits and cleaves open into

booming crumbling walls that jar the ground: then the perfect
ice spheres from the high world come down in a bounding
rustle, some remnants of thunder far along the periphery

grumbling: lightning strikes close and lightbulbs sear
in their sockets and flick out: then the heavy rain brushes
in on wind gusts at the windows: a drenching too demonstrable

105

for poppies, all twenty-eight heads half-closed with bending
over and drooping: for a long time the eaves-gutter,
lightening, keeps a mesh of seed-ice, the milky cores:

because of the holdings of its many needlepoints, every one
drop-bulbed, the long shags of the blue spruce lie into one
another like shoals of high moss and a weatherless shower

ticks on for hours after rain: slowly the boughs lighten,
loosen, jar and sprinkle apart: a thousand acres of those
trees could suspend a shower and turn it into an all-day

soak: that would be good for the brooks whereby the rocks
had refused all but a wetting: mediations soften the
extremities without changing their quantities, merely

106

translating times: getting to know your philosophy, finely
rational and small, is like coming into a city and finding
a trellis, precise, consistent, which after all only holds

up a bush: some people when they get up in the morning see
the kitchen sink, but I look out and see the windy rivers
of the Lord in the treetops: you have your identity when

you find out not what you can keep your mind on but what
you can't keep your mind off: mind, many sided, globe-like,
rich with specification and contrariety, is secure from

slogans, fads, starved truths, and propaganda—defeats itself,
meanwhile shoring itself up with sight and insight: how to
devise a means that assimilates small inspirations into a

107

large space, network, reticulation complex (almost misleading)
but moved forward by a controlling motion, design, symmetry,
suasion, so that harmony can be recognized in the highest

ambience of diversity: in a single day, one may "hear" a small
connection, an interesting phrase, but to what can each day's
stock be added: what is the measure to accommodate the

diverse impressions, moods, intuitions: in the right scope
any fragment fits: since we can't, apparently, have whole
motions of mind through the higher reaches (sufficiently

impregnated with the concrete), we turn to the unit to
represent the universal: but while we can hope to arrive at
the definition of essence through the unit, we can never in

108

that way satisfy the other capacity of the mind to achieve
definition by ordered accumulations, massive suasions: if
nothing shaped stays and shapelessness is dwellingless, where

can we dwell: as shapes (bodies) we dwell only in the flow
of shapes, turning the arcs of mortality: but the imagination,
though bodiless, is shaped (being the memory or imagined

memory of shapes) and so can dwell in nothingness: the human
being is as inscrutable and unformulable as a poem, or, if
possible, more so: the gas station attendant has a bottomless

well in him, too—shoots from his brain down his spine, breaks
into incredible ramification, the same as bottomless: we
have our definitions, imperfect, but all we have: around them,

109

though, and running through, and immensely more vast, the
indefinable, the source of possibility: acme came: speaking
with "the flower of the mind" gets pollen up my nose: how

to give up the life of words for life: just now (June 6 in
the dusk) only a few dozen flowers are left on the honeysuckle
bush, the flowers like the pink, sprung mouths of tiny vipers:

thunder shakes pennies out of stack: if one follows the western
littoral of Africa northward, one moves up past Walvis Bay
to Sorris Sorris and, rounding out westward and turning back

in again, to Benguela and Lobito and then way on up, swerving
out again slightly westward, to Port Gentil and then sharply
west to Cape Palmas and on up and around to Sidi Ifni and

110

past the gaping Strait and on up past Oporto and, crossing
water, to Brest and then through certain colder finaglings
one turns into the other side of the world along Siberian

shores to the Bering Strait and, switching, descends along
the western littoral of North America: if all else fails,
try hocus-pocus to bring your writing into focus: for sun,

moon are out of joint until you bring them to a point: cry
Muse! and if you cannot reach her, bleed some juice from a
writing teacher: bad images are bad but what is worse is

verse loose where it should be terse: verse would be, except
for magic, dull as life and twice as tragic: the shortest
route to adulation is to skirt your education: in need to be

111

diminished, I sought out peaks and stars and at my cost
sang them high and bright: you don't have to be superhuman
to survive—let go and let your humanity rise to its natural

height, said the star, and you will in that smallness be as
great as I: so I sat down and sang and mountains fell and
at last I knew my measurable self immeasurable: the weak

rigs a universe against himself, then overstrives to keep
himself—but nothing is set up, nobody cares, it's all right
for him to come out, shine a little and love his light:

aspirations (misdirections) move in the upper branches of
the mind like vine vipers, slender, loopy, slithery:
notice the highest cranes reach into the deepest pits:

112

therefore, if my slat-steel triangulations of abstraction
and strict cables surprise and dismay you on the landscape,
think how from under the foundations the waters of life

may rise to meld with mirrors and wave the cranes away:
think of that: for such the elegance of my uprisings: what
is deep to come to, being overlaid with too much stone of

fear, suggests high drills: the little red squirrel dashes
out onto the thin branches, picks a maple seed, and dashes
back to the cover of bigger branches: nibbles out the

greenmeal seed then drops the wing into asymmetrical flutters,
not the nosewing-spin of the true event: semblance with no
journey: terrors bluster with undercutting sweeps, or pelt

113

with staying fragmentation (hail on the spring garden) through
or in the mind, the swirlings of imbalanced loops between
highs and lows, just like weather predictions and actual

storms over average landscapes: one terror mind brings on
itself is that anything can be made of anything: if there are
no boundaries that hold firm, everything can be ground into

everything else: the mind making things up, making nothing
of what things are made of: scary to those who need prisons,
liberating to those already in: that this dismissal is

possible, no more recalcitrance within or without, slides our
surfaces and disturbs our deeps: the poppies are all gone:
the tulips were all gone last week: we have lemon lilies now,

114

some iris, some spirea still white where it's mostly brown: we
have four hills of mound-building ants: two hills are on the
lawn and regularly get their hills sliced off: one hill is

under the four-legged merry-go-round: I have to clip under
there so I leave it alone: one mound is just between the
blacktop and shrubs, on a slight incline, so it's safe from

the lawnmower: I notice the ants have two primary visible
duties: some ants bring little dried bits, castings from maple
bloom, dried strips of grass, even green clover leaves and deposit

them on top of the mound: meanwhile, other ants bring up pellets
of soil, and a weaving betwixt them takes place which the rain,
short of destroying, glues and seals: they are interesting ants:

115

I was pulling veronica out of the lawn when this hornet came
up upon my squatted self, buzzed around my anklebones inquiringly
and then buzzingly persisted about my face and neck: that was

a few days ago: then he did it the next day: and the next: but
today when he did it, I retreated into the house: he followed me
and got caught between the door and the screen: the screen door

was ajar and when he got in the groove, I closed the door crushingly:
I took him by the wing to the mound builders: they hassled him
down the side part way, for some reason, and commenced to pierce

and suck him: I am sorry, of course, but the veronica has to
be pulled, as I don't want to use funny sprays that might poison
the worms and birds: killing to save perplexes: just facts,

116

just bits: let's, as if sore, grab a few things from the flood,
from the imagination's burning everything up into the contours
of staying: or let us, before the transfusions commence, hamper

the imagination with full freightages of recalcitrance, cripple
it short of any transmutation that avoids the massive registration:
if the burn's to be true, let it be the real: nor let us guide

too much the proceeding but be carefully in it when it goes: we
must come out on the other side, on our feet and ready to ride:
this drawn fellow said he was quartered, split two ways,

horizontally and vertically, by the horizontal into height and
depth and by the vertical into left and right: said he tried
to live in one half only to find it halved: these terrible

117

partitions interested him in unity: he wanted all of himself
together but each quadrant felt defiant and exclusive: he
looked for the coordinate only on finding it to find it

represented by zero: a terrible bind that made him at least
attentive: very much aware, he could give many sides to any
argument: we all thought that largeness a spark of divinity:

we told him everything has a cost but he rejoined he would
settle for something less expensive: the poem insists on
differences, on every fragment of difference till the fragments

cease to be fragmentary and wash together in a high flotation
interpenetrating much like the possibility of the world: the
poem wants every fragment clear but a fragment until, every

118

fragment taken into account, the fragments will be apprehended
to declare a common reality past declaration: a fragment is
a person, edgy with difference, fearful of broadsweep

elimination: interpenetration is a welling up of fresh deeps
of tolerance and consideration: I beg the liberty of such
edges and wells to function and of fearful concision to relax

its boundaries inclusively: if one would preserve the integrity
of his going, his taut conveyance (bright and trim), he must
be willing to give over to indirection: if in the South

Atlantic one selects the prime meridian as an ideal northward
voyage, one runs into difficulty in the progression: at Accra
or thereabouts one must abandon ship and hire elephants or

119

Fiats and proceed at a lumbering or sizzling pace: and
somewhere around Upper Volta it will be necessary to get
camels ready (and do something with the elephants, put them

in keep for the return trip or dispose of them by sale,
shot, or wilderness), packed with figs, dates, and curd,
and around Oran find a marketplace to trade the spitting

camels off for ships again, a short voyage, and then onto
land: before ships again, there will be dogsleds and
finally seals slipping off chunks of sea-ice: bend out

and around and in in order to keep familiar rudder and sail
at hand: when poetry was a servant in the house of religion,
it was abused from all angles, buggered by the fathers,

120

ravished by the mothers, called on to furnish the energies
of entertainment (truth) for the guests, and made, at the
same time, a whipping-post for the literal: poetry is not

now a servant in the house of religion, the matter having
become clear who got what from which: if you wish to get
religion now you will have to come and sit in poetry's

still center, bring your own domestic help, and resort to
your own self-sustainment: if, leaving center, you make
uses of poetry, you must represent them as uses, not as the

true life, and in recognition of that you must dress your
uses in rags as an advertisement that violations are underway:
no more hocus-pocus derived from images and lofty coordinations:

121

if you want to drain a place, don't begin on the marshy side:
you'll get your feet wet and every time you trench, water will
run in hiding your trench depth: begin on the other side

of the clog where the ground may be crumbly dry and where you
can work without sloshing and then you can at last break into
the water and see it start from dead holding into motion's

declarations and extensions: if you do everything with
economy and attention, the work itself will take on
essentialities of the inevitable, and you will be, if causing,

participating in grace: the aspects will concur in one motion:
when the water breaks into the trench, notice spells of
jerking in the water's head, caused by the uneven angles and

122

depths of shoveling: but soon the water will find a smooth
current compensating for the ragged edges, and you may feel
that the water itself, as if grateful, is joining to complete

your work: attention enters in: I can't understand my readers:
they complain of my abstractions as if the United States of America
were a form of vanity: they ask why I'm so big on the

one:many problem, they never saw one: my readers: what do they
expect from a man born and raised in a country whose motto is *E
plurisbus unum:* I'm just, like Whitman, trying to keep things

half straight about my country: my readers say, what's all
this change and continuity: when we have a two-party system,
one party devoted to reform and the other to consolidation:

123

and both trying to grab a chunk out of the middle: either we
reconcile opposites or we suspend half the country into
disaffection and alienation: they want to know, what do I

mean *quadrants,* when we have a Southeast, Northeast, Southwest,
and Northwest and those cut into pairs by the splitting
Mississippi and the Mason-Dixon line: I figure I'm the exact

poet of the concrete *par excellence*, as Whitman might say:
they ask me, my readers, when I'm going to go politicized or
radicalized or public when I've sat here for years singing

unattended the off-songs of the territories and the midland
coordinates of Cleveland or Cincinnati: when I've prized
multeity and difference down to the mold under the leaf

124

on the one hand and swept up into the perfect composures of
nothingness on the other: my readers are baffling and
uncommunicative (if actual) and I don't know what to make of

or for them: I prize them, in a sense, for that: recalcitrance:
and for spreading out into a lot of canyons and high valleys
inaccessible to the common course or superhighway: though I

like superhighways, too, that tireless river system of streaming
unity: my country: my country: can't cease from its
sizzling rufflings to move into my "motions" and "stayings":

when I identify my self, my work, and my country, you may
think I've finally got the grandeurs: but to test the center
you have to go all the way both ways: from the littlest

125

to the biggest: I didn't mean to talk about my poem but
to tell others how to be poets: I'm interested in you, and
I want you to be a poet: I want, like Whitman, to found

a federation of loveship, not of queers but of poets, where
there's a difference: that is, come on and be a poet, queer
or straight, adman or cowboy, librarian or dope fiend,

housewife or hussy: (I see in one of the monthlies an astronaut
is writing poems—that's what I mean, guys): now, first of
all, the way to write poems is just to start: it's like

learning to walk or swim or ride the bicycle, you just go
after it: it is a matter of learning how to move with
balance among forces greater than your own, gravity, water's

126

buoyance, psychic tides: you lean in or with or against the
ongoing so as not to be drowned but to be swept effortlessly
up upon the universal possibilities: you can sit around

and talk about it all day but you will never walk the tightwire
till you start walking: once you walk, you'll find there's
no explaining it: do be afraid of falling off because it is

not falling off that's going to be splendid about you, making
you seem marvelous and unafraid: but don't be much afraid:
fall off a few times to see it won't kill you: O compatriotos,

sing your hangups and humiliations loose into song's
disengagements (which, by the way, connect, you know, when
they come back round the other way): O comrades! of the

127

seemly seeming—soon it will all be real! soon we will know
idle raptures (after work) leaning into love: soon all our
hearts will be quopping in concert: hate's fun, no doubt

about that, tearing things up and throwing them around and
ending some: but love is a deep troubling concern that rises
to the serenity of tears in the eyes: prefer that: hold

hands: help people: don't make a big fuss and embarrass
them, and if your empathy is right you won't, but help people
where the message is that it's called for: and when you're

tired out, write songs about hate's death and love's birth:
you'll get it straight, you'll see: the mind, a periscope
in the perilous scope, rises from comforting immersions in

128

what sways good and feels fine, the plush indulgences like
ledges or canyon scarps rimmed with spring's finery of bush,
the creams and jellies of reverie, and looks abroad for a

reassuring scope to sweetness or for the oncoming, if
distant, catastrophe that will return it to the pudding
of change, the mind's own describing and roving fire

drowned from shapening: the mind studies the soil, wedges
out spudeyes and plants them, attends, devours with its body,
and yet declares itself independent of the soil: like a

Portuguese man-of-war, the mind shakes rustling tentacles
down into the nutriment: it wants to survive: as storms
of zooplankton pour up onto the shelf at dusk, it swarms

129

to feed: (I want to be declared a natural disaster area:
I want my ruins sanctioned into the artifice of ruins: I
want to be the aspect above which every hope rises, a

freshening of courage to millions: I want to be, not shaved
marble in a prominence that cringes aspiration, but the
junkyard where my awkwardnesses may show: my incompletions

and remains tenable with space: I want to be the shambles,
the dump, the hills of gook the bulldozer shoves, so gulls
in carrion-gatherings can fan my smouldering, so in the

laciest flake of rust I can witness my consequence and times:
I want to be named the area where charlatan rationality comes
to warp, where the smooth finishes bubble and perk, where

130

aerosol deodorants lose their breath: when the freeze of
this century retreats, leave me the slow boulders and
smashed pebbles arbitrarily disposed: whatever was bright,

clever, chic, harmonious in my time took plane from mind's
tricky shallows and too quickly found plastic rightness
distant from the winding center: declare me an area

prohibited where the wind can come among the grasses and
weeds, robins nest in high wheels under the whole look of
heaven:) chaos, pushed far, gives up chunky sleaziness and

in the milling mastication of change assumes pale light
in a diffusion and on the periphery gives off golden
illuminations of unity and, beyond, becomes the merciful,

131

non-instrumental continuum: the continuum allows at the
outermost thinnings skimpy weavings tearing into the surrounding
uterus of nothingness, a way to go: from this womb

separations appear, the land from water, the sky departs
upward, the water breaks up into seas, lakes, rivers, runlets,
a few noticeable configurations, short of perplexing multeity:

the mind rides the cycle from all things enchanted and
summoned into unity, a massive, shining presence, to all
things diffused, an illimitable, shining absence, confusion

the wrong zone of intermediacy, a lack of clarifying extremes:
the week of windy cold comes and removes the last hangers-on
from the trees and heaps them against hedge, fence: rake

132

the leaves or a still morning's inch of snow will weight
every disposition disposed, the pheasant moving about dazzled
with the sudden loss of ground: I am like the earth about

twenty-three degrees off, which gives me summer and winter
moods, sheds hopes and sprouts them again: what are my hopes:
it's hard to tell what an abstract poet wants: my hopes

are for a context in which the rosy can keep its edges out of
frost: my hopes are for a broad sanction that gives range
to life, for the shining image of nothingness within which

schools of images can swim contained and askelter: my hopes
are that the knots of misery, depression, and disease can
unwind into abundant resurgences: forces other than light

133

give shadow: the leaves under the maple tree are flattened
in an overlapping elliptical, headed southward, the sun
itself subsided southward: after a long northwind, the leaves

are the wind's shadow: a solid shadow with no shadowing
leaves on the tree, just northward splinters of nakedness:
a shadow of former substance transmigrated into shadow-substance,

not shadow but a redisposition of substance: the redisposition's
form is the shadow of all the redisposing forces, a shadow
of the universe! a record and perfect summary, signs of

gusts in scatterings-out at the shadow tip: I wonder if one
can pay too much attention, as one can pray too much and
forget to shop for dinner: legible, the evidences propose

134

no text: dwelling over ashes, the bitter, spent spirit recovers
the taste of desertion, the sense of scripture: meanwhile,
in calm, a thousand shows wind to manifestation and a thousand

others loosen ropes and take down their poles: how much
attention can we pay, count the snowflakes or flurries, the
clouds or blue intervals: is celebration to pay no attention

but go along with the ongoing, buoyed up by accuracies
beyond receipt: if geese can see low, the leaf shadow will
show them which way to go: light patches on the floating

hill across the lake stand up into columns when half a
snow-flurry, giving medium, brushes through: interpenetrations
of gray and blue with breaking luminescences, streamings

135

skirting whirls: the column stands but moves over the hill,
the foot walking up and down ravines, and sometimes leans
a broken top as if held up by the sun: time enough to think

of death when there's no time left to think: big ditties:
the poem is love: love is fictional only where it can't
grow, but always supreme: making the poem makes the body

that makes love: the abstract poem reaches too far for the
body, love bodiless there, better, if scarier, burns nearby:
or having loved nearby, the abstract poem turns to the spirit,

bodiless and frightless: or the abstract poem, searching
breadths and heights of fiery ease, trains its way down to
settle in the woman's eye: we have so many ways to go wrong

136

and so often go wrong, we must read rightness written in the
face of wrong: if the abstract poem goes out and never
comes back, weaves the highest plume of mind beyond us, it

tells by its dry distraction, distraction: love is better
awry than any other quantity true: the abstract poem, yearning
into the lean-away, acquires a skeleton to keep it here, and

its jangling dance shocks us to attend the moods of lips,
the liquid changes of the spiritual eye: the abstract poem
cleaves through the glassy heights like the hump of a great

beast, the rising reification, integration's grandest, most
roving whale: in this way Enlil became a god and ruled
the sky: in this way earth became our mother: in this way

137

angels shaped light: seek the whole measure that is ease
and ramble around without constriction or distortion
(debilitating exclusion) until the big sky opens the freedom

between design and designed airiness: the rational mind
absorbed, structures float in plenitude rather than in
starved definition: order, the primeval hillock, is a

lessening from chaos, chaos the ampler twin: the visible
resides within the invisible: the coherent within the
incoherent: the discontinuous, the discrete, occurs within

the continuous: the visible, coherent, discrete dwell
in flotation which faces out on the illimitable: the power,
he said, to invent and sustain great structure is uncommon,

138

dibs and dabs, driblets and tail-ends defeating minds, those
incapable of the see-through intermingling: but there are
minds, he maintained, nervous of structures, especially the

impressive, minds requiring the see-through to act as liquid
of flotation outside the structures, such a flotation no
structure could hem in but many structures could sort out

their destinies fairly freely in: I don't know about you,
but I'm sick of good poems, all those little rondures
splendidly brought off, painted gourds on a shelf: give me

the dumb, debilitated, nasty, and massive, if that's the
alternative: touch the universe anywhere you touch it
everywhere: man's a scourge not because he is man but because

139

he's not man enough: how public like a smog publicity is:
in spite of the spectacularity of the universe (even in the
visual reception) it appears to those who have gone above our

atmosphere that the universe is truly a great darkness, light
in the minority, unsurrendered coals sprinkled in the thinnest
scattering, though, of course, light, even when seen from

afar, attracts the attention most: but out on the periphery
the lights are traveling so fast away their light can't get
back to us, darkness, in our dimension, finally victorious

in the separation: I have dreamed of a stroll-through, the
stars in a close-woven, showering bedazzlement, though
diamond- or ruby-cool, in which I contemplated the universe

140

at length: apparently, now, such dreams, foolish anyway,
must be abandoned and the long, empty, freezing gulfs of
darkness must take their place: come to think of it, though,

I'm not unfamiliar with such gulfs, even from childhood, when
the younger brother sickened and then moved no more: and
ahead lies a gulf light even from slow stars can never penetrate,

a dimension so endless not even the universal scale suits it:
the wise advise, don't get beyond yourself into foolish largeness,
when at my step is a largeness the universe lies within:

to be small and assembled! how comforting: but how perishable!
our life the tiny star and the rest, the rest: this extreme
flotation (it and us) this old, inconstant earth daily born

141

new into thousands of newborn eyes—proceeding by a life's
length here and there, an overlapping mesh of links proceeding:
but, for me, turning aside into rust, reality splintering the

seams, currents going glacial and glassy with knowledge, the
feared worst become the worst: meanwhile, once again the world
comes young, the mother follows her toddler around the cafeteria

and can't see him her eyes so keeping in touch with the admiring
eyes of others: (the old mother, thin-white, thicked-jawed, feels
her way, but barefooted, out to the mailbox: nothing: all

the fucking finished, all the sweet, terrifying children grown
up and blown away, just the geraniums in the tire watered
every day, fussed at, plucked:) let me tell you how I get up

142

in the morning: I get up, take a step or two, and morning jars
and pauses me, and I look down into the bottom of my grave:
shaken, I move, though, as if through iron, on when my life,

my real life, wakes up in a tantrum and shakes me like last
year's beanstakes: I lean against the doorjamb until my life
gags into despair, and then I proceed: I proceed, how, into

what: I say, if I can get through this hour, I won't come to
another one but to life: with a front left, I erect a smile
on it, and right away everybody starts laying his troubles on me:

I say in myself, don't lay any more trouble on me: when here
comes another youth anxious for fame and sorry he doesn't
have it: what can I do, he says: well, I say, why not try

143

whatever you can: by the time you amount to something,
the people you meant it to mean something to are dead and you
are left standing there, your honors in your hands: the

ribbons wilted: the cheese melted: the sausage running:
there at the end (which may be anywhere) after dullish
afternoons and vacant mornings, after settlement from the

disturbance of sex, when you were coward, clown, fool, and
sometimes lord, there saved for the end, a novelty, death,
infinite and nonrepeating, an experience to enter with

both eyes wide open, the long play that ends without boredom:
its unexpectedness such you don't have the materials for
a rehearsal, more surprising than with girls where one

144

approach run through can profit a later one: you go in,
your mouth stretches so wide it turns you inside out,
a shed skin, and you gulp nothingness, your biggest bite,

your greatest appetite, stuffed with vacancy: who knows
whether in the middle years, after the flashing passions
seem less like fountains and more like pools of spent flood

metal, one may not keep on partly because of that black sucker
at the end, mysterious and shiny: my skull, my own skull
(and yours) is to be enclosed—earpits, eye sockets, dangled-open

mouth—with soil, is to lie alone without comfort through
centuries and centuries, face (if any) up, as if anticipating
the return of the dream that will be only the arrival of

145

the nova: how sluggish consciousness, when in death the
nova is a wink away! the rational, the formed, defined,
directional is the male principle: the cushioner, the female

principle, the pudding within which the rational plays:
these two principles give birth to mind: one could not want
all pudding (pudenda) nor all shape but an interworking,

a whole generating: this poem is an elongated cylinder
designed to probe feeling, recognition, and realization,
to plunder the whoozies of the world sensationally and cause

to come to bear what is and may be: I am not a whit manic
to roam the globe, search seas, fly southward and northward
with migrations of cap ice, encompass a hurricane with

146

a single eye: things grown big, I dream of a clean-wood
shack, a sunny pine trunk, a pond, and an independent income:
if light warms a piney hill, it does nothing better at the

farthest sweep of known space: the large, too, is but a
bugaboo of show, mind the glittering remnant: things to do
while traveling: between entrance and exit our wheels

contact the ribbon of abstract concrete: speed-graded curves
destroy hills: we move and see but see mostly the swim of
motion: distance is an enduring time: here, inside, what

have we brought: between blastoff and landing, home and
office, between an event of some significance and another
event of some significance, how are we to entertain the time

147

and space: can we make a home of motion: there is a field
of sheep, vanishing: something terminal may be arriving to
that house, but we are leaving: mortgage payments, water rent,

phone bills, medical insurance, steep steps imprisoning an old
man: but we are fueled and provisioned: motion is our place:
history lists and you know by the difficulty of getting around

at an angle all day that something is too much or amiss: your
awareness begins to take shape, to obtrude, to call attention to
itself, a warp or persisting tension: you are reminded

to go below and check the ballast: how is it that what was
enough for both sides has become too much for one side and not
enough for the other: you gather a force and go down to make

148

correction: history uprights, sways to the give and take in
a touchy balance, so active, lively, so responsive: nevertheless,
a wind may come up subtle or sudden and persist and you may

have to go down and change the ballast, only to find when the
wind does cease that uprightness in an imbalance is imbalance:
fire, instructive flame, foliate saprophyte, consumer,

criticism at the wafered edges of form, master of shape, god
of a kind, traveling wave of the imagination, fire line,
waster of the old that gives destruction's ash to the future,

we are assembled, what is the instruction: the instruction is
in perceiving the principle itself, the god, his action: by
this instruction we are reduced, our works ashes in the wind,

149

but the field, gone through, is open and in the woodburn
the jackpine cone flicks open and ejects seed: ferns rouse
subsoil curls: birds accept the brush margins of feeding

grounds and hawks police the new actions for waywardness:
the gods of care and economy of motion, the grass gods, the
god of the killdeer arrive, and the old god of the forest

begins to take everything away again: from other planets,
as with other planets from here, we rise and set, our presence,
reduced to light, noticeable in the dark when the sun is

away: reduced and distanced into light, our brotherhood
constituted into shining, our landforms, seas, colors
subsumed to bright announcement: we are alone in a sea that

150

shows itself nowhere in a falling surf but if it does not
go on forever folds back into a further motion of itself:
the plenitude of nothingness! planets seeds in a coronal

weaving so scant the fabric is the cloth of nakedness:
Pluto our very distant friend skims a gulf so fine and far
millions and thousands of millions of years mean little to—

how far lost we are, if saving is anywhere else: but light,
from any distance or point we've met it, shines with a similar
summation, margin affirmational, so we can see edges to the

black roils in the central radiances, galaxies colliding in
million-year meetings, others sprung loose into spiral
unwindings: fire, cold space, black concentration:

151

harmonies (in my magnum hokum) I would speak of, though
chiefly as calling attention to neglected aspects of fairly
common, at least overreaching, experience: with considerable

rasping along the edges, bulgings of boundaries, we made
and tamed into play each of these States: if the States
kept falling into lesser clusters about lesser points of

focus (and then the long division, so costly), still we
checked and balanced and, incorporating as much sin as grace
with each holding, kept the mobile afloat, together, each

dangle with good range to dip and rise and convey itself
roundly with windy happenstance, communicating, though, its
position throughout the network and receiving from the sums

152

of the network just adjustments: yes, we got it all together,
ocean to ocean, high temperate to low temperate, and took
in so much multiplicity that what we hold person to person

in common exists only in the high levels of constitution or
out to the neighbor's fence, an extreme, an extreme pity,
with little consolidation in the middle after all: still,

it holds and moves within the established rigors: now, with
the same rasping and groaning, we try to put the nations and
communities of nations together and there, too, only by

joining tenuous extremes, asserting the dignity of the single
person above united nations: we pray this may succeed and
correct much evil in the dark edges of dislocation and

153

distraction: lately, we've left out the high ranges of music,
the planetary, from our response, though the one sun is here
as usual and the planets continue to obey holy roads: the

galaxy is here, nearly too much to speak of, sagely and
tremendously observing its rotation: we do have something to
tune in with and move toward: not homogeneous pudding but

united differences, surface differences expressing the common,
underlying hope and fate of each person and people, a gathering
into one place of multiple dissimilarity, each culture to its

own cloth and style and tongue and gait, each culture, like
the earth itself with commonlode center and variable surface,
designed-out to the exact limit of ramification, to discrete

154

expression into the visible, specific congruence of form and
matter, energy moving into the clarification of each face, hand,
ear, mouth, eye, billions: still with the sense of the continuous

running through and staying all the discretions, differences
diminished into the common tide of feelings, so that difference
cannot harden into aggression or hate fail to move with the

ongoing, the differences not submerged but resting clear at
the surface, as the surface, and not rising above the surface
so as to become more visible and edgy than the continuum:

a united, capable poem, a united, capable mind, a united capable
nation, and a united nations! capable, flexible, yielding,
accommodating, seeking the good of all in the good of each:

155

to float the orb or suggest the orb is floating: and, with the
mind thereto attached, to float free: the orb floats, a bluegreen
wonder: so to touch the structures as to free them into rafts

that reveal the tide: many rafts to ride and the tides make a
place to go: let's go and regard the structures, the six-starred
easter lily, the beans feeling up the stakes: we're gliding: we

are gliding: ask the astronomer, if you don't believe it: but
motion as a summary of time and space is gliding us: for a while,
we may ride such forces: then, we must get off: but now this

beats any amusement park by the shore: our Ferris wheel, what a
wheel: our roller coaster, what mathematics of stoop and climb: sew
my name on my cap: we're clear: we're ourselves: we're sailing.